WOMEN IN SCIENCE AND ENGINEERING

Tu
YOUYOU

BY M.M. EBOCH

ILLUSTRATED BY ELENA BIA

Rourke
Educational Media

A Division of
Carson Dellosa
Education

ROURKE'S
SCHOOL to HOME
CONNECTIONS
BEFORE AND DURING READING ACTIVITIES

Before Reading: *Building Background Knowledge and Vocabulary*

Building background knowledge can help children process new information and build upon what they already know. Before reading a book, it is important to tap into what children already know about the topic. This will help them develop their vocabulary and increase their reading comprehension.

Questions and Activities to Build Background Knowledge:

1. Look at the front cover of the book and read the title. What do you think this book will be about?
2. What do you already know about this topic?
3. Take a book walk and skim the pages. Look at the table of contents, photographs, captions, and bold words. Did these text features give you any information or predictions about what you will read in this book?

Vocabulary: *Vocabulary Is Key to Reading Comprehension*

Use the following directions to prompt a conversation about each word.

- Read the vocabulary words.
- What comes to mind when you see each word?
- What do you think each word means?

Vocabulary Words:
- awards
- fame
- persevered
- priority
- recipes
- research
- responsibility
- wring

During Reading: *Reading for Meaning and Understanding*

To achieve deep comprehension of a book, children are encouraged to use close reading strategies. During reading, it is important to have children stop and make connections. These connections result in deeper analysis and understanding of a book.

 Close Reading a Text

During reading, have children stop and talk about the following:

- Any confusing parts
- Any unknown words
- Text to text, text to self, text to world connections
- The main idea in each chapter or heading

Encourage children to use context clues to determine the meaning of any unknown words. These strategies will help children learn to analyze the text more thoroughly as they read.

When you are finished reading this book, turn to the next-to-last page for **Text-Dependent Questions** and an **Extension Activity**.

TABLE OF CONTENTS

SICKNESS AND HEALTH

Tu Youyou was born in China. Her father got her name from an old Chinese poem. The poem says, "The deer cry yoo yoo" as they eat wormwood. Wormwood is a wild plant.

Youyou's family knew education was important. Youyou and her four brothers went to good schools.

Chinese Names
In China, family names, or last names, are said first. The child's given name is said second. Tu was the family's name.

At 16, Youyou got very sick. She had to leave school for two years. When Youyou finished high school, she knew what she wanted to do. She wanted to cure diseases like the one she had. She would study medicine in college.

Youyou studied traditional Chinese medicine. Traditional Chinese medicine uses many medicines made from plants. It has been around for more than 3,500 years. Youyou learned how plants can treat diseases. She also studied modern medicine. She saw how both can work together.

China had a problem with a disease called malaria. Two early cures stopped working. Scientists around the world looked for new cures. They tested over 240,000 plants, animals, and minerals. None of them worked.

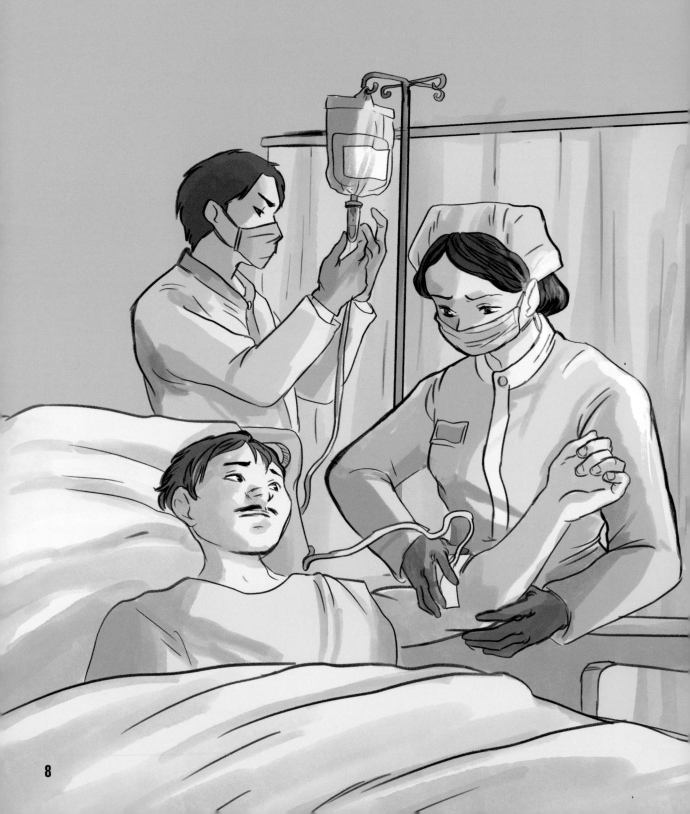

Insects with Disease
People can get malaria from mosquito bites. Malaria makes people very tired. They may sweat or feel cold. They can be sick for years.

ANSWERS IN OLD BOOKS

Chinese leaders started a **research** group called Project 523. They would look for cures in traditional Chinese medicine. Youyou was an expert in both traditional Chinese medicine and modern medicine. They asked her to lead the group.

This was an honor but also hard. Youyou had two young daughters. She knew she wouldn't have time to give her daughters the care they needed. She had to ask other people for help with her daughters. Youyou focused on her work.

"The work was the top **priority**," she said later. "I was willing to sacrifice my personal life."

Youyou and her team looked for **recipes** in traditional Chinese medicine. They thought an old recipe could be the key to a new way to cure malaria. They talked to Chinese medicine doctors. They read books written long ago. In three months, they found 2,000 recipes.

The group started testing these recipes on animals with malaria. They tried many plants, minerals, and animal parts. Nothing worked.

Youyou had a book written in 340 A.D. She looked for new recipes. One recipe used sweet wormwood. The same plant from the poem where Youyou got her name!

The book said sweet wormwood treated fevers that came and went. Malaria caused fevers. Could wormwood cure malaria?

The team tested the parts of the plant, but nothing worked. Youyou went back to the ancient recipe. It said to put the plant in water. Then "**wring** out the juice and drink it all."

The researchers were boiling plants to make medicine. Maybe high heat was causing the problem. Youyou did new tests with lower heat.

Her team worked long hours every day. They made lots of samples to test on animals. After two years of hard work, sample number 191 finally stopped malaria!

Would the medicine work on people? Would it hurt them?

Youyou and two others on her team took the medicine. **"As the head of the research group, I had the responsibility,"** Youyou said. They waited in the hospital. What would the plant do to them?

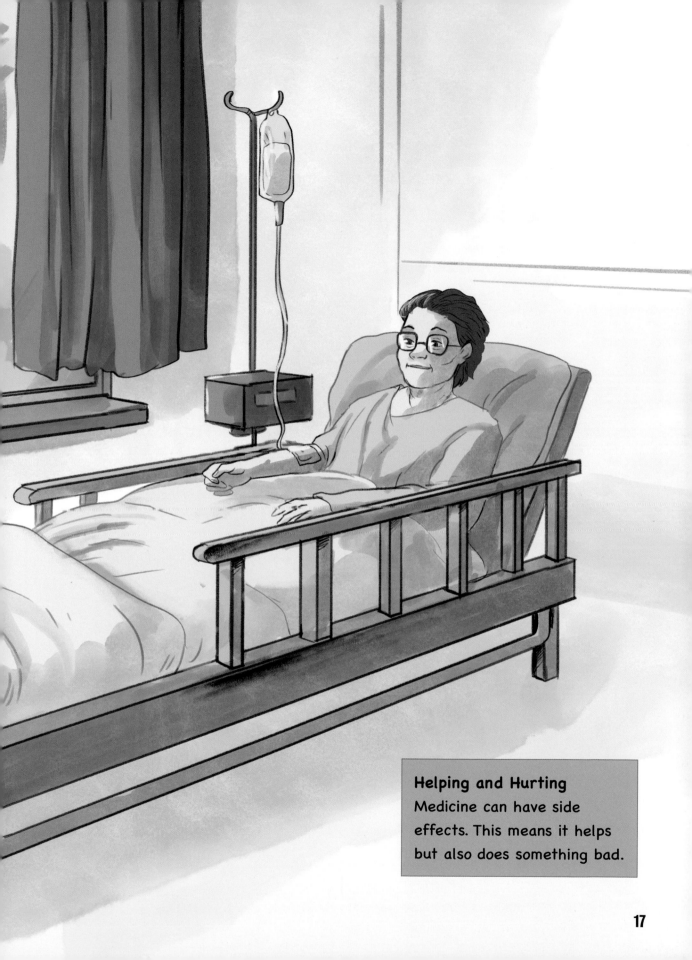

Helping and Hurting
Medicine can have side effects. This means it helps but also does something bad.

SAVING LIVES

The medicine did not hurt them. Next they tried it on 21 people with malaria. Everyone got better. Over time, the medicine saved many lives. Youyou called it "a true gift from old Chinese medicine."

Youyou tried and failed many times before she solved the problem. She **persevered** until she found a medicine that worked. Youyou mixed old medicine with new science. That way, she found a new cure.

Youyou got many **awards** for her work. In 2015 she won a Nobel Prize in Physiology or Medicine. That is one of the biggest honors in the world.

She said she did not want **fame**. She wanted to do something that helped the world. She showed how ancient medicine can help us today.

Youyou hopes more young people will study science and help others. "As long as you work hard, you will make achievements," she says.

TIME LINE

340: Ge Hong writes *A Handbook of Prescriptions for Emergencies*.

1930: Tu Youyou is born on December 30.

1951: Youyou begins to study at Peking University in Beijing, China.

1955: Youyou graduates from Beijing Medical College at age 24. She starts work at the China Academy of Traditional Chinese Medicine.

1967: China starts Project 523 to find a new cure for malaria.

1969: Youyou is made head of Project 523.

1972: Youyou reports on her successful malaria treatment.

1972: Sweet wormwood is tested on malaria patients.

1973–1990: Youyou is head of the chemistry department at the China Academy of Traditional Chinese Medicine.

2009: Youyou publishes a book about her career in science.

2015: Youyou gets the Nobel Prize in Physiology or Medicine. She is the first person from mainland China to get a Nobel Prize in a science category. She is 85 years old.

GLOSSARY

awards (uh-WORDZ): prizes or honors for special achievements

fame (fame): to be well known by many people

persevered (pur-suh-VEERD): to have continued to do or tried to do something

priority (prye-OR-i-tee): put first because it is very important

recipes (RES-uh-pees): lists of things to mix for making food or medicine

research (ree-SURCH): the careful study of something to learn about it

responsibility (ri-spahn-suh-BIL-i-tee): a duty one must perform, such as a job or chore

wring (ring): to twist and squeeze tightly in order to remove liquid

INDEX

TEXT-DEPENDENT QUESTIONS

1. Why did Youyou leave school for two years?

2. What is traditional Chinese medicine?

3. Where did Youyou find a recipe to treat malaria?

4. What did Youyou's team have to do before sick people could use the medicine?

5. Youyou was named after a poem. How did this poem connect to her life later?

EXTENSION ACTIVITY

What does your family do when someone is sick or hurt? Do you drink hot tea or eat chicken soup? Does this help? Does that make it a medicine? With an adult's help, look at your family's kitchen and bathroom. What foods, herbs, or spices might help your health? Are there traditional medicines you use?

ABOUT THE AUTHOR

M.M. Eboch also writes books as Chris Eboch. She likes to write about science and history. Her novel The Eyes of Pharaoh is a mystery in ancient Egypt. The Well of Sacrifice is an adventure about the Maya. She lives in New Mexico with her husband and their two ferrets.

ABOUT THE ILLUSTRATOR

Elena Bia was born in a little town in northern Italy, near the Alps. In her free time, she puts her heart into personal comics. She loves walking on the beach and walking through the woods. For her, flowers are the most beautiful form of life.

www.rourkeeducationalmedia.com

Quote sources: Celia Hatton, "Nobel Prize winner Tu Youyou helped by ancient Chinese remedy," BBC News, Beijing (October 6, 2015): https://www.bbc.com/news/blogs-china-blog-34451386; "Chinese Woman Wins Nobel Prize for Discovering Artemisinin," Women of China: http://www.womenofchina.cn/html/special/19053166-1.htm; "Tu Youyou – Biographical," NobelPrize.org., Nobel Media AB 2020, (2015): https://www.nobelprize.org/prizes/medicine/2015/tu/biographical/; "TU YOUYOU: Nobel Prize in Physiology or Medicine in 2015," The Nobel Foundation: https://www.nobelprize.org/womenwhochangedscience/stories/tu-youyou

Edited by: Hailey Scragg
Illustrated by: Elena Bia
Interior design by: Alison Tracey

Library of Congress PCN Data

Tu Youyou / M.M. Eboch
 (Women in Science and Technology)
ISBN 978-1-73164-329-2 (hard cover)
ISBN 978-1-73164-293-6 (soft cover)
ISBN 978-1-73164-361-2 (e-Book)
ISBN 978-1-73164-393-3 (ePub)
Library of Congress Control Number: 2020945049

Rourke Educational Media
Printed in the United States of America
01-3502011937

Tu Youyou

Tu Youyou is a unique scientist. She is an expert in traditional Chinese medicine and modern medicine. When China needed someone to solve their problem with malaria, Youyou was the perfect person for the job. She mixed old medicine with new science and saved many lives. Her story inspires young people to enjoy science.

Alignment

This book supports the C3 Framework for Social Studies State Standards. Readers will learn about women who have shaped historical changes in the fields of science and technology.

Books in the series *Women in Science and Technology* include:

Ayanna Howard

Rachel Carson

Maryam Mirzakhani

Tu Youyou

Annie Easley,
Elizabeth Blackwell,
Grace Hopper,
Katherine Johnson,
Mae C. Jemison,
Megan Smith

ISBN-13: 978-1-73164-293-6

Guided Reading Level: **P**

Rourke
Educational Media
rourkeeducationalmedia.com

A Division of
Carson
Dellosa
Education